DISCARDED

W9-AQH-326

GRIFFINS

Thanks to our adviser for her expertise, research, and advice:
Elizabeth Tucker, PhD.
Distinguished Service Professor
English, General Literature and Rhetoric
Binghamton University, Binghamton, NY

Editor: Shelly Lyons
Designer: Hilary Wacholz
Art Director: Kay Fraser
Production Specialist: Kathy McColley

Picture Window Books are published by Capstone
1710 Roe Crest Drive, North Mankato, Minnesota 56003
www.capstonepub.com

Copyright © 2020 by Picture Window Books, a Capstone imprint. All rights reserved.
No part of this publication may be reproduced in whole or in part, or stored in a
retrieval system, or transmitted in any form or by any means, electronic, mechanical,
photocopying, recording, or otherwise, without written permission of the publisher.

Library of Congress Cataloging-in-Publication data is available
on the Library of Congress website.
ISBN 978-1-5158-4444-0 (hardcover) | ISBN 978-1-5158-4448-8 (ebook pdf)

Summary: Is that a lion? Is it an eagle? NO, it's a griffin, the winged king of beasts!
Glossy feathers, powerful wings, and the body of a lion make up this fantastical
creature. Ever wondered what a griffin eats? Where does it live? Wonder no more!
Striking illustrations and matter-of-fact text take you on a noble journey to learn all
about griffins.

All internet sites appearing in back matter were available and accurate
when this book was sent to press.

Printed and bound in the USA.

PA71

GRIFFINS

BY MATT DOEDEN

ILLUSTRATED BY MARTIN BUSTAMANTE

A treasure hunter creeps up a rocky slope.
A cave opens into the mountain. It holds a large
treasure of gold and jewels. Something stirs within.
A loud screech echoes off the cave walls.

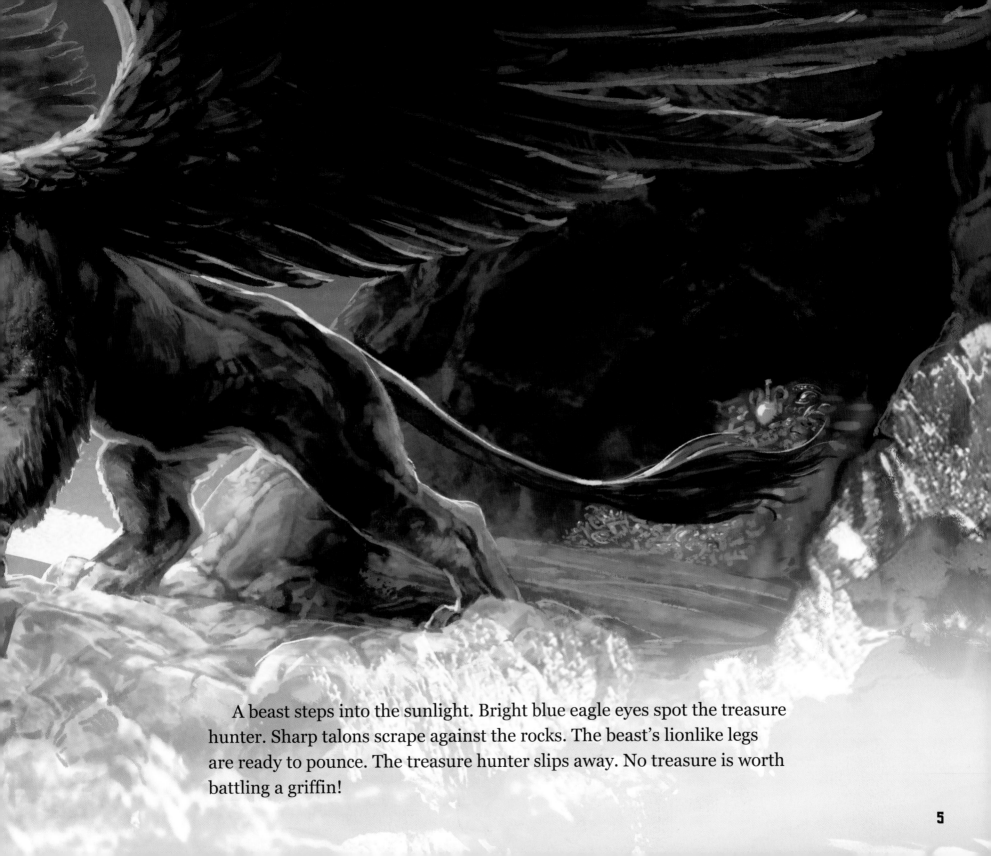

A beast steps into the sunlight. Bright blue eagle eyes spot the treasure hunter. Sharp talons scrape against the rocks. The beast's lionlike legs are ready to pounce. The treasure hunter slips away. No treasure is worth battling a griffin!

GRIFFIN BEHAVIOR AND LIFE CYCLE

Griffins are beasts of myth. They have the head, wings, and front legs of an eagle. They have the body of a lion. These creatures like to live alone. But they gather to mate.

EGG

HATCHLING

Like eagles, griffins hatch from eggs. A female lays a clutch of around three eggs. Each egg is about 6 inches (15 centimeters) long. The female watches over the eggs until the baby griffins hatch.

The mother brings food such as mice to the nest. But the young griffins must fight for what she brings. A young griffin that is too weak will starve.

YOUNG GRIFFIN

ADULT GRIFFIN

Adult griffins may grow to the size of an adult lion. As they get bigger, they seek out larger prey. Griffins are deadly hunters. They can even kill horses!

7

Griffins are carnivores. Much like eagles, griffins must leave the nest. Each griffin must find its own hunting area. Young griffins steal food from adults. They also hunt for small animals and fish.

NORTHERN GRIFFIN

GRIFFIN FEATURES

There are two main kinds of griffins. A Northern griffin is more eagle-like.
An Indian griffin is more lionlike. But all griffins are similar. Many griffins
have the body, legs, and tail of a lion. Sometimes a griffin's tail is a snake.
A griffin is sleek and powerful.

INDIAN GRIFFIN

A griffin's eagle eyes see everything. Its eyesight is at least five times sharper than a human's sight. A griffin can spot prey from high in the sky. Watch out!

A griffin's wings are powerful. The wings are covered in feathers. Long ago, some people believed a griffin's feathers were magical. Of course, getting a feather from a griffin was a dangerous task!

14

A griffin uses its sharp beak and talons to grasp prey.
Most griffins have eagle talons on their front feet. But Indian
griffins may have the front paws of a lion. These griffins use sharp
lion claws in much the same way.

PARTS OF A GRIFFIN

EYES

A griffin has powerful eagle eyes.

BEAK

The hooked beak is sharp and strong.

FEATHERS

Magical feathers help the griffin in flight.

TALONS

Long, curved talons can easily grab prey.

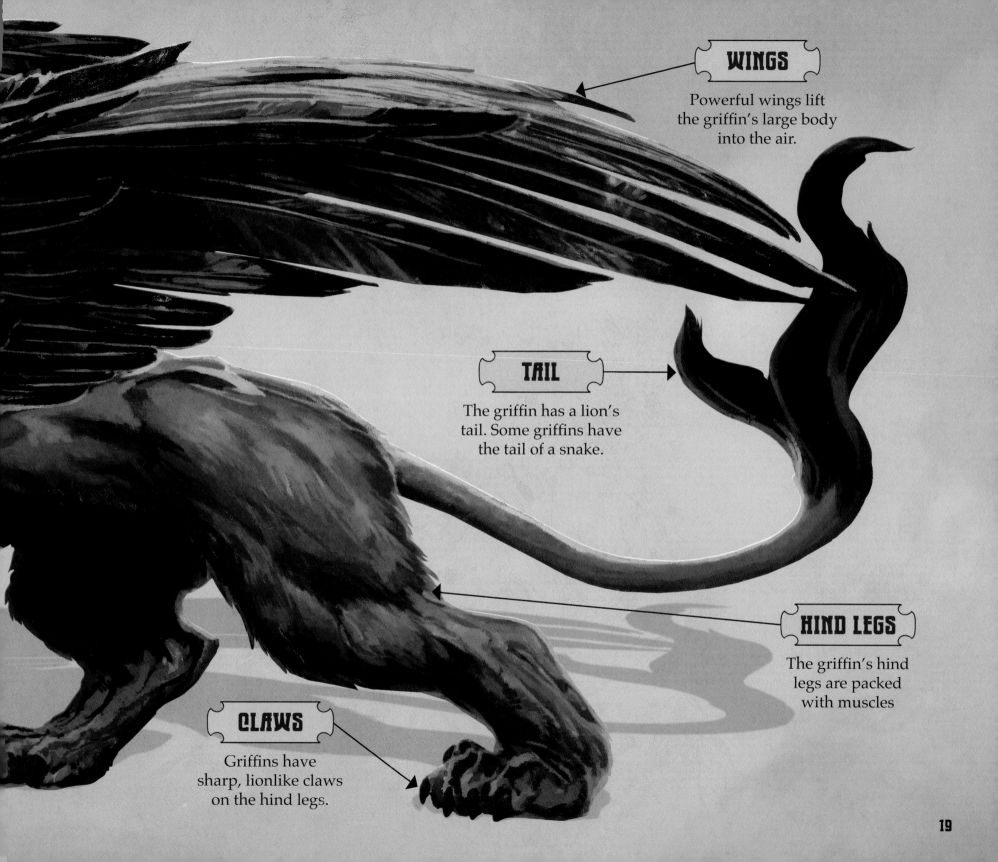

WINGS

Powerful wings lift the griffin's large body into the air.

TAIL

The griffin has a lion's tail. Some griffins have the tail of a snake.

HIND LEGS

The griffin's hind legs are packed with muscles

CLAWS

Griffins have sharp, lionlike claws on the hind legs.

GRIFFINS OF MYTH

In stories, griffins are often symbols of good in the world. In Ancient Greek and Roman stories, griffins are symbols of power and wealth. Griffins are strong and loyal in all things and are best known for guarding treasure.

Griffins live on in myths and stories today. Popular fantasy authors
Mercedes Lackey and Larry Dixon wrote about them in their books,
The Black Gryphon, *The White Gryphon*, and *The Silver Gryphon*.

There are creatures that are similar to griffins. The popular *Harry Potter* series, by J.K. Rowling, has a hippogriff. It has the body, hind legs, and tail of a horse. Its front legs, wings, and head are like an eagle's.

The legend of these powerful beasts lives on. In fact, people may still look up to the sky in the hopes of spotting a griffin in flight!

ABOUT THE AUTHOR

Matt Doeden began his career as a sportswriter. Since then he's spent almost two decades writing and editing hundreds of children's fiction and nonfiction books. *Darkness Everywhere: The Assassination of Mohandas Gandhi* was listed among 2014's Best Children's Books of the Year from the Children's Book Committee at the Bank Street College of Education. Doeden lives in Minnesota with his wife and two children.

ABOUT THE ILLUSTRATOR

Martin Bustamante is an illustrator and painter from Argentina. At the age of three he was able to draw a horse "starting by the tail", as his mother always says. As a teenager, he found in movies like *Star Wars* and books like *Prince Valiant,* by Harold Foster, new and fascinating worlds full of colors, shapes, and atmospheres that became his inspiration for drawing. He started working as a professional illustrator, and has worked for several editorials and magazines, from Argentina to the United States to Europe.

GLOSSARY

ancient—from a long time ago

carnivore—an animal that eats only meat

clutch—a group or nest of eggs

Indian—from the country of India

mate—to produce offspring

myth—a traditional story, often from ancient times

pounce—to jump on something suddenly and grab it

prey—an animal that is hunted by another animal for food

slope—a slanted surface; one end is higher than the other end on a slope

symbol—something that stands for something else

talon—an eagle's claw; a talon has four toes, each with a very sharp curved nail

wealth—lots of money

CRITICAL THINKING QUESTIONS

1. Griffins are part lion and part eagle. Can you think of two other animals you could mash together? What would that new animal's powers be like?

2. What body parts make griffins good hunters? Think of another wild animal. What body parts help it to survive?

3. Can you think of a story in which a griffin might help a character in some way? What would the griffin do?

READ MORE

Loh-Hagan, Virginia. *Griffins*. Magic, Myth, and Mystery. Ann Arbor, Mich.: Cherry Lake Publishing, 2018.

Marsico, Katie. *Beastly Monsters: From Dragons to Griffins*. Monster Mania. Minneapolis: Lerner Publications, 2017.

Sautter, A.J. *How to Draw Griffins, Unicorns, and Other Mythical Beasts*. Drawing Fantasy Creatures. Mankato, Minn.: Capstone Press, 2016.

INTERNET SITES

Animal Planet: Wild Animals, Top 10 Mythical Animals
http://www.animalplanet.com/wild-animals/10-mythical-creatures/

Ducksters: Ancient Greece, Monsters and Creatures of Greek Mythology
https://www.ducksters.com/history/ancient_greece/monsters_and_creatures_of_greek_mythology.php

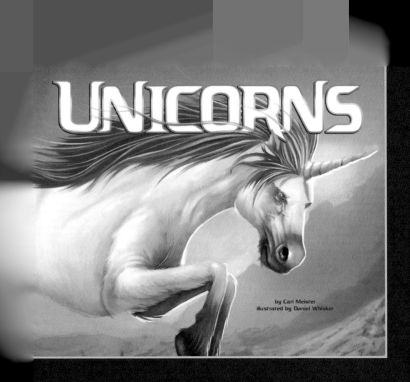

UNICORNS

by Cari Meister
illustrated by Daniel Whisker

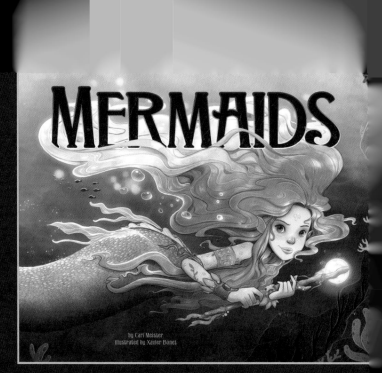

MERMAIDS

by Cari Meister
illustrated by Xavier Bonet

DRAGONS

by Matt Doeden
illustrated by Martin Bustamante

GRIFFINS

BY MATT DOEDEN
ILLUSTRATED BY MARTIN BUSTAMANTE